Francis Scott Key
and "The Star-Spangled Banner"

by Lynea Bowdish · Illustrated by Harry Burman

Photo Credits: P. 31 (Fort McHenry): © Roger Miller/H. Armstrong Roberts;
p. 31 (lyrics): Tom Pantages photo/courtesy LOC

For information contact:
MONDO Publishing
980 Avenue of the Americas
New York, NY 10018

Visit our web site at http://www.mondopub.com

Printed in the United States of America

02 03 04 05 06 07   9 8 7 6 5 4 3 2 1

ISBN 1-59034-038-8 (PB) ISBN 1-59034-195-3 (HC)

Library of Congress Cataloging-in-Publication Data

Bowdish, Lynea.
  Francis Scott Key and "The Star-Spangled Banner" / by Lynea Bowdish ; illustrated by
Harry Burman.
    p.cm.
  ISBN 1-59034-195-3 -- ISBN 1-59034-038-8 (pbk.)
    1. Baltimore, Battle of, 1814--Juvenile literature. 2. United States--History--War of
1812--Flags--Juvenile literature. 3. Flags--United States--History--19thcentury--Juvenile
literature. 4. Key, Francis Scott, 1779-1843--Juvenile literature. 5. Star-spangled banner
(Song)--Juvenile literature. I. Burman, Harry, 1954- II. Title.

E356.B2 B69 2002
                                                                        2002067790

All across the United States of America, people sing a song called "The Star-Spangled Banner." They sing it at the beginning of baseball games. They sing it at school.

"The Star-Spangled Banner" is the national anthem of the United States of America.

"The Star-Spangled Banner" was written in 1814 by Francis Scott Key. He was a lawyer from the state of Maryland. He also liked to write poems.

In 1814, the United States was fighting a war against the British. It was called the War of 1812. The United States was losing the war.

The British had burned the Capitol Building and the

President's House in Washington, D.C. President James

Madison and his wife, Dolley, had left the city.

British ships were on their way to attack the
city of Baltimore.

An American named Dr. William Beanes was a prisoner on one of the British ships.

Dr. Beanes was friends with Francis Scott Key.

Francis went out to the British ships. He wanted the British to let Dr. Beanes go.

Francis showed them letters written by British soldiers.

These soldiers had been hurt in battles. Now they were prisoners of the American army.

The letters were about Dr. Beanes. The soldiers were thanking Dr. Beanes for taking care of them.

The British agreed to let Dr. Beanes and Francis go—
but not until after the attack on Baltimore.

They did not want Dr. Beanes and Francis to warn

the American army about the attack.

On September 13, 1814, the British attacked Fort McHenry. The fort is just outside of Baltimore.

17

Francis and Dr. Beanes had to watch the battle from a small ship.

They could see the huge American flag flying over the fort.

All day long, the British bombed Fort McHenry. The soldiers at the fort fired back.

That night, rockets lit up the sky. There was a lot of noise. Francis watched from the ship. Who was winning? He just couldn't tell.

Early on the morning of September 14, the battle stopped.

It got very quiet. Francis watched the sun come up.

The smoke cleared. Francis saw a flag on the fort. Whose flag was it?

It was the United States flag! The Americans had won the battle.

Francis was very happy. He wrote a poem about what he
saw and what he felt. The poem fit the music of a song he knew.

Francis and Dr. Beanes were set free. They went back
to Baltimore.

Francis's poem was printed in the newspaper in Baltimore.

Soon, everyone was singing it. They called it "The Star-Spangled Banner."

SEPTEMBER 20, 1814

Defense of Fort McHenry

The Star-Spangled Banner

O say, can you see, by the dawn's
early light,
What so proudly we hailed at the
twilight's last gleaming?
Whose broad stripes and bright
stars, through the perilous fight,
O'er the ramparts we watched, were
so gallantly streaming?

And the rockets' red glare, the
bombs bursting in air,
Gave proof through the night that
our flag was still there.
O say, does that star-spangled
banner yet wave
O'er the land of the free and the
home of the brave?

In 1931, Congress made "The Star-Spangled Banner" the United States' national anthem.

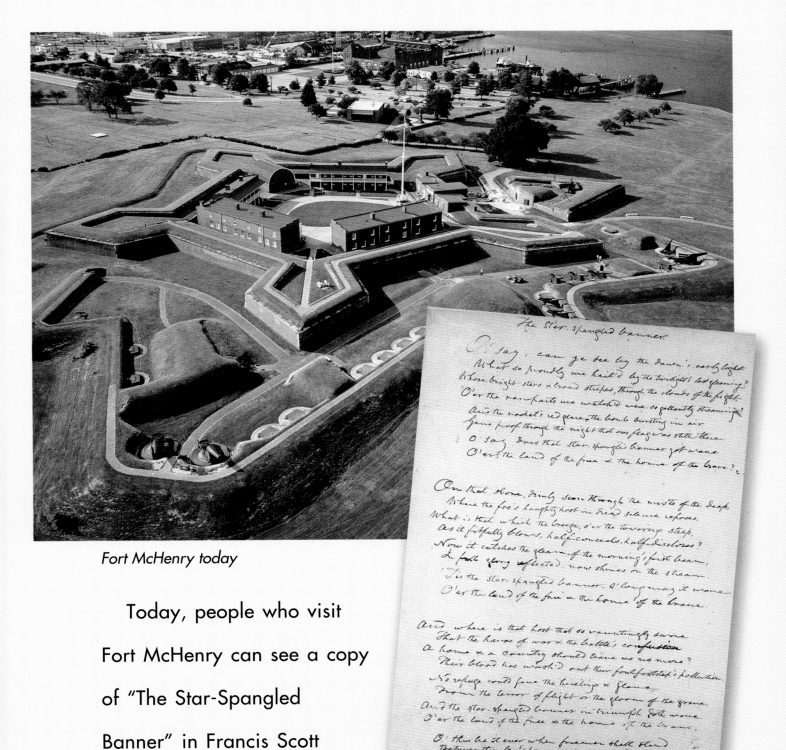

Fort McHenry today

Today, people who visit Fort McHenry can see a copy of "The Star-Spangled Banner" in Francis Scott Key's handwriting.

The Star-Spangled Banner

Words by Francis Scott Key
Music by John Stafford Smith

Arrangement by Kathy Boyd

O' – say can you see, by the dawn's ear-ly light, what so

proud-ly we hail'd at the twi-light's last gleam-ing? Who's broad

stripes and bright stars thro' the per-il-ous fight, o'er the

ram-parts we watched, were so gal-lant-ly stream-ing? And the

rock-et's red glare, the bombs burst-ing in air gave

proof thro' the night that our flag was still there. O'

say does that star span-gled ban-ner yet wave, O'er the

land of the free and the home of the brave?